ENCOURAGED TO FINISH

STAYING FOCUSED ON THE RACE

Kimberly Robinson Green

Creative Unity Publishing

Encouraged to Finish

Copyright © 2015 by Kimberly Robinson Green

ISBN 978-0-9822796-5-6

Library of Congress Control Number: 2015958418

Cover Design: Donna Osborn Clark at CreationsByDonna@gmail.com

Layout and Interior Design: www.CreationByDonna.com

Editing: Shell Vera at eyesstraightahead@gmail.com

Published by: Creative Unity Publishing
www.CreativeUnityPublishing.net

Scripture quotations used in this book are from
THE HOLY BIBLE, King James Version , KJV and
THE HOLY BIBLE, NEW INTERNATIONAL VERSION®, NIV® Copyright
© 1973, 1978, 1984, 2011 by Biblica, Inc.® Used by permission. All rights
reserved worldwide.

Merriam-Webster. (2015) www.merriam-Webster.com

Manufactured in the United States of America

First Edition

This book is dedicated to my Dad (Lee E. Robinson Sr.) gone but never forgotten. To my family and close friends for believing in me, encouraging me, and always speaking life over me. It takes a special group of people to be great cheerleaders to support someone else. You know who you are. You are all my blessings from the Heavenly Father and I will forever cherish and honor you. Thank you!

Acknowledgments

This book is a result of many prayers and a lot of time. In addition to the energy, endurance, and victory God has given me to complete this work, there are some special folks who surrounded me with the support I needed to ensure I could complete this task with grace and humility. I'd like to give special thanks to my amazing husband, David Green Sr. my backbone in all that I do; my three sons: David Jr, Dezmond, and Daniel Green. Daniel thank you for helping mom out with this last project, encouraging and giving me your marketing ideas (wink). To my mother, Mrs. Christine Robinson; thanks mom for everything. And my two brothers, Cliff and Lee Robinson Jr, I can always depend on you. Thank you all this couldn't been done without you! To my Graphics Artist and friend Donna Osborn Clark, Thank you for your guidance in this business, words can't explain how much I appreciate your support. God bless you! Special thank you to my editor Michelle Vera, you are amazing and a God send.

Table of Contents

How I Started My Race

Encouraged to Finish was placed on my heart years ago. I thought to myself, "What a beautiful title, but me Lord?" Being a shy city girl, I wasn't sure what direction God wanted me to take but I knew I should write – so I did. I'm glad that I heard His voice, was obedient to His command, and was encouraged to start. Sometimes I can be my worst critic (can't we all?) but loving God made it easy for me to lace up my shoes and start the race that would become this book.

As you enter into your race – or reenter it, I pray each page will provide you with tools to enhance your lives. This book is meant to encourage and empower you if you are ready for hope, change, and God's will to be reactivated – or activated – in your life. While I am not an expert in life, I have been through many experiences that empower me to say, "God's been faithful and good to me." I know that there is nothing too hard for our God and that He loves you no matter what you have done or ever will do. I feel blessed and honored to be a vessel for His Kingdom and to be the one chosen to write this book to encourage you!

I'm convinced that you're here for a reason. God's creations are all beautiful; therefore <u>you are beautiful</u>. I imagine that some of you have been in a place where it seems your only solution is to throw in the towel; but I have to tell you, "It's not over until God says it's over!" To succeed, you must understand who you are and what you possess internally. Once you realize that who you are is vital to God's kingdom, you will be able to embrace His purpose for your life! God's way is the only way; surrendering to His perfect will for your life is beneficial to us all! God's mercy and grace is there to cover us regardless of how difficult it may be, and His favor is better than life. Don't give up, you can make it!

I pray as you read this book, you will feel more empowered to press forward and not allow the enemy or others' negativity to discourage you. The Bible says, "Greater is He that is within me than He that is within the world" (1 John 4:4 KJV). God's love will be there to get you through; don't lose focus on your goals. Be encouraged to finish what He has started within you.

Why You Need to Prepare to Run

"Therefore, since we are surrounded by such a great cloud of witnesses, let us throw off everything that hinders and the sin that so easily entangles. And let us run with perseverance the race marked out for us." **Hebrews 12:1 NIV**

Look at the picture to the right. Now imagine that you are on the race track running this race called life and you are coming upon this sign and all of the hurdles in your way. This is how many of you feel daily: as though you can't encounter a lane free of distraction or hurdlers. You become overwhelmed and want to give up because the distractions seem too much to jump over or avoid.

What do you do when you feel this way? Do you choose to continue or do you quit? If you choose to quit, you are choosing the seemingly easiest way out. I get it; I've wanted to do that many times too (and have done it on several occasions). We all possess an innate amount of perseverance that can be overridden easily when life causes us to want to throw in the towel.

Look at the image again and notice the sign on the first hurdle. The hand gesture commands your attention; the color red notifies the brain to stop any action. Thankfully, we don't have to submit to the gestures and meanings of ALL signs that life puts in front of us. If you choose to continue the race despite seeing hurdles, or even falling, you've made the right choice!

Sometimes overcoming the hurdles of life can seem too high of a goal to reach, but it's within you to do so. Oftentimes, the very hurdle that may cause you to fall can be the same one that lifts you up. The trials, hurdles, hurts, disappointments are all part of God's plan to help you grow to become who He has made you to be and to draw closer to Him! Do you not know that God sees within you what you possess and all of the gifts He has placed within you? You must continue. Don't allow those hurdles to make you fall. Use them as a greater source to move ahead!

It's Time to Start Your Race

"Do you not know that in a race all the runners run, but only one gets the prize? Run in such a way as to get the prize. Everyone who competes in the games goes into strict training. They do it to get a crown that will not last, but we do it to get a crown that will last forever."
1 Corinthians 9:24-25 NIV

Our lives mirror a race. As runners run, they must remain mentally and physically able to address the intense hurdles placed before them because their goal is to run past their opponents and finish the race as victors. Can you see yourself running in this race called life? Have you had to jump some hurdles along the way? Have you fallen and had to get back up? Have you sometimes felt like you had to start all over again? It seems like the finish line is so far away, but, like that runner, you must complete the task regardless of how hard it may be. You may get tired and grow weary, but your reward is awaiting you!

Anything worth having is worth fighting for. Do you feel like you are worth it? Do you have goals, dreams, and visions only you can bring forth? We often give the devil credit for everything that goes wrong. But sometimes it isn't he who is holding you back; it's you not wanting to admit the greatness within you because you feel unworthy or inadequate. The enemy of your soul realizes that if he can discourage you from moving forward, he will succeed in stopping the powerful impact you will have on the world!

It is important for you to understand that you play a big part in God's plan. You may be asking yourself, "Plan for what?" God has a master plan! Just as a coach desires for his team to succeed, God wants to ensure you are fully equipped to complete the assignments given to you in this life. He has given you special talents and abilities that make you specifically qualified to complete each assignment He will give to you. Just as the coach would ensure you are surrounded by the right teammates, God will bring people into your life who He needs you to work with to ensure you complete that tasks He has given you. You are not alone. You have all you need to prepare to run this race – and finish it. Take a moment to look around so you can determine your assignment, those placed within your life to help you complete it, and the hurdles before you that you must strategically overcome.

Triumph over Discouragement

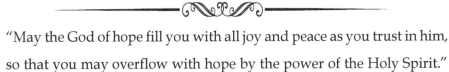

"May the God of hope fill you with all joy and peace as you trust in him, so that you may overflow with hope by the power of the Holy Spirit."
Romans 15:13 NIV

As you begin to go after your goals, complete your assignments, and conquer your fears, the enemy will throw several obstacles your way. Just as the sprinter will face hurdles as he or she competes, the devil will ensure you are faced with several distractions and hurdles to conquer. Discouragement is one of these hurdles.

Discouragement is an ugly factor that lingers and latches on to us. It thrives on our down days. It causes us to believe we can't pursue or complete a task. It laughs at us when we fail and applauds us when we quit! Discouragement is not in our corner nor is it our friend.

When we want to believe in miracles, it provides reason to doubt. When we are ready to step out, discouragement tells us to get back in the boat. It steers us towards unbelief, discontentment, and apathy. It makes us suspicious about whom to believe or whom to let in to our lives. Discouragement pulls at our heart strings and tells us that no one cares and no one loves us. It encourages emotions such as anger and bitterness. Being discouraged creates stress in our lives. But I have good news for you: you can defeat the feeling of discouragement!

Triumph over discouragement by calling forth the hope within you. Hope is the light when you're in a dark place in your life; it tells you to go forward when you're scared. Hope speaks life into your dead situation and allows you to dream as if you were experiencing success. Hope encourages you to smile when you feel like crying; laugh when you feel like yelling, and lend a helping hand when you feel like withholding a closed fist. Hope defeats depression, encourages happiness, and inspires true joy to take residence in your heart. It calms your spirit and gives you peace. Hope brings a smile to your face and tells you can make it. Hope is in Jesus Christ!

You will experience discouragement often if you are being called to do something big for the Lord. I believe many of you reading this book have some mighty dreams that God has breathed into your life and wants you to see become reality within the next few years. But you are scared, and maybe rightfully so. Hope is what you go to when you don't have the faith to move past the obstacles in your path. It is what calls forth what is not as though it is and breathes new life into your situation. Hope…reach deep down, pull it out, and grab onto it as you retie your shoes and become encouraged to finish your race.

Be Patient

"And now, Lord, what do I look for? My hope is in you."
Psalms 39:7 NIV

To hear God's plan you must be still and listen. In today's society, it seems like there's not enough time to steal away into a quiet place to listen to anything. It is easy to move God to the back burner because you know He is always there. But He wants to be the center of everything you do -big or small- and for you to hear His direction. This is the only way you can endure and conquer things ahead!

Your Heavenly Father is your number one fan. He believes in you and loves you unconditionally. It's not easy to trust and believe when things go wrong; but if you trust and depend on God, He will lead you in the way you should go (Proverbs 3:5).

If God didn't think that you could make it He wouldn't give you the task. He wants you to depend upon Him and understand that you can do all things He gives to you (Philippians 4:13). Faith is the key to unlocking your true potential; just a small measure of faith can carry you a long way! You don't have to understand everything, but you have to place your trust in God and know that He won't ever let you down!

How many times you've been promised something and it didn't happen? How often has someone given you her word and you believed her, only to be let down? How many times have others lied about you, talked about you, or spoken down to you? I know that you can all identify with let downs, broken promises, and backstabbing. The great news is that you serve a God who does not commit any of these acts! He will not break promises and He certainly will not let you down.

God allows things to take place. He puts certain people in your lives to shake the boat a little. You have to endure some pain, uncertainty, some weak moments, and even some setbacks. Why? Because this is how you move forward. These experiences teach you what and whom to allow into your lives the next time around – and, more specifically, what and whom you should NOT allow into your lives.

While all runners receive the satisfaction of completing the race, only a few will walk away with the coveted medals given to first through third place. In this race we call life, compete as though you expect to win a medal and stand upon the platform celebrating your victory. Walk as though you already know you will win instead of as though you feel unqualified to have started.

Don't Quit

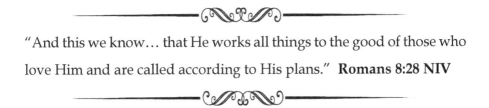

"And this we know… that He works all things to the good of those who love Him and are called according to His plans." **Romans 8:28 NIV**

For you to be reading this book, chances are pretty good that you are hanging on by a thread. You may be feeling battered and beaten, wondering where God went and why He won't come back and save you. You may feel like you started walking out your faith and stepped into the oceans like the songs and pastors have all encouraged you to do, only to find yourself treading water and calling out like David did, "My God, my God. Why have you forsaken me?" (Psalm 22:1). You need a break and you need it yesterday.

Maybe you are not happy with your job. Maybe you are tired of being single. Maybe your marriage is ready to break down if you don't do something dramatic to change it. Every month the bills add up, the tensions mount within various relationships in your life, and you feel more alone than you have ever felt in your life. Your teenagers aren't listening. Your husband is cheating. Your boss is ready to fire you. You feel like God is nowhere to be found. It feels like life can't get any worse and it will never get any better. Maybe picking up this book was your last attempt to try to stay in this life before giving up altogether.

Listen closely to what I say here: Life can and will throw you curve balls. They are going to come daily, weekly, and monthly. If you aren't experiencing them, you may want to ask the Lord if you are truly in the right position because the enemy doesn't need to attack what he does not feel threatened by (and truthfully, he should feel threatened daily by those living out God's plans). But there is hope! You can triumph over those curve balls. You can defeat the enemy. You can conquer all obstacles in your path (2 Corinthians 12: 8-10).

You must understand that God has a plan for you. That plan may be very different from the plan you have for yourself; in fact, most times it is. You have to be still and hear the Spirit's leading and listen to the Lord's heart. What is He saying to you? What is His will for your life? To truly live in a position of overcoming the obstacles, you must be attentive to His will and leading, open to His correction, and walk daily according to His commandments. To demonstrate this fact, I want you to think about a mother and her child. Let's look at that relationship as though you are a mother:

As a new mother, you give everything to your baby. You nurse him, love him, care for him, and support him as he develops. You teach him to walk, eat, and use the facilities. You demonstrate love and respect for others, tell him the sky is the limit, and remind him that he can do any thing he sets his mind to do. You give him all the tools he needs to succeed and ensure his environment is the best possible. As he grows, you wonder whether he will do and remember all you have taught him.

Seemingly overnight, your son becomes an adult and no longer needs you daily. Over the years, he has become more independent, began doing some things that you didn't have planned for his life, and sometimes seems to be a man you don't know. But nothing about your love for him changes. In fact, your love grows stronger with each new day. When you look at him, you realize that you would lay down your life if it meant he could accomplish all you have believed for him. You know him inside and out. You want to direct his paths but realize that you cannot do so unless he offers the invitation.

You stand on the sidelines and cheer him on, even when life seems to have dished him exactly what he deserved in the moment. You want to run to his aid and help him up but restrain yourself from doing so because you know what is best for him. Instead, you remind him you are there for him and hold out your hand until he comes to you and says, "Mom, I need help. Will you help me?" And when he comes to you and says those words, you reach out with arms wide open and say, "Of course."

A mother's love for her child and God's love for us are not as different as we sometimes believe. We love because God first loved us (1 John 4:19). In the scenario above, the mother had a plan for her child whether she acknowledged it or denied it. She set forth a series of intentions that she desired her son to walk out. But she couldn't make him take the paths she set out for him. This is exactly what God does for you.

God has a plan for your life, but you must choose whether you will walk it out or give up. The entire time you are deciding which choice you will make, He is there empowering you for success and trying His best to keep you from failure. He is standing there with arms wide open waiting for you to ask Him for help, to seek His plan and learn how you can accomplish it. He wants you to accept His offer to help you succeed in life. But God took a step most mothers will never have to take: He demonstrated His unconditional love to the point of sacrificing His Son, who laid His life down for us that we may forever live (John 3:16).

Many times we want to give up because relationships become broken or don't work out as we wanted them to. Our expectations for situations are different from the reality we live out. But I am here to encourage you that your success is not dependent upon your relationships with others, how they view your successes or failures, or whether your reality and expectations align. No! Your success is dependent upon how well you listen to the Father's heart, hear His voice, and follow His instruction. He has given you all you need to succeed and is standing there cheering you on as you walk out your faith and run the race of life. Don't quit! Instead, look to the One who gave you these plans and ask Him how to move forward.

Hang on to God

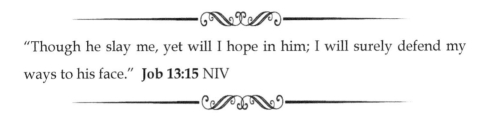

"Though he slay me, yet will I hope in him; I will surely defend my ways to his face." **Job 13:15** NIV

There are many times when quitting will seem to be your only option. In those moments, it is best to hang on to God and pray that He gives you the strength to walk through the temptation or struggle (1 Corinthians 10:13). Please allow me to share with you one of my experiences.

Several years ago, I encountered a situation in my family business that caused me to want to throw in the towel and find a new path for my life. I was a new business owner – young and naive. My mother became ill, which did not align with the deadlines I was facing. In this business, there were specific papers that needed to be filed within detailed parameters or else the business was considered out of compliance. During her illness, someone made an error while completing the paperwork. Though my mother was the one person I knew who could fix anything pertaining to business, I couldn't go to her because I feared it would negatively affect her health.

I felt alone despite the support of my staff. While they were available and willing, they were limited on what they could do about the situation. One day, we received a visit that resulted in terrible news. I learned that things didn't look good and there was not much I could do to change that fact.

At that moment, I couldn't call on anyone but God. I cried out, "Lord, I don't know what to do or which direction to take. Can you please direct my steps?" I needed help quickly and I knew only God could provide it. I cried for many days and nights. My husband and closest friends prayed on my behalf. I was doing all I knew how to do and asking for support where I knew to ask for it.

I felt hurt, alone, and as though I had failed those around me and myself. I remember my niece Alex saying to me, "T, just pray. I don't know how but God will work it out!" Just when I thought it was over and we were going to lose everything, God stepped in and worked everything out. The Bible says the prayers of a righteous person are powerful and effective (James 5:16b).

A little over a month later, I received a call from the same folks who had visited me previously and they noted that I was pulling myself up and things were looking good. PRAISE GOD! I am humbled and blessed to report to you that our family business is now running better than ever! Doors have been opened that no man can close (Revelation 3:7-8). God has since blessed us with a brand new building that better benefits the business than before. The favor of God is over my life and all praises belong to Him!

This situation was not easy and I really thought I had reached my end. But God had other plans. I had to go through this test so God could show me I had the tools to pass it. When the next test comes, I can remind myself what He's already done and have that confidence that He will do it again! You can do the same. Right now, I want you to say aloud, "Congratulations [Your name]! You are pulling yourself out of this and you will succeed!" Say these words any time you doubt that God is able. These are the words He wants to say to you because He is with you and empowering you to pull yourself through.

Your Dreams are Worth the Wait

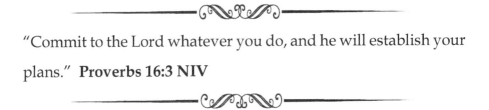

"Commit to the Lord whatever you do, and he will establish your plans." **Proverbs 16:3 NIV**

When I was growing up, one of my dad's favorite meals to cook was Shrimp Fried Rice and Robinson Burgers. He would take his time cooking the fried rice until the flavors blended perfectly! There were several ingredients he added to make this dish, but the pride he took in ensuring the best flavor and presentation was worth the time he had taken to make it. Daddy was a chef at heart and enjoyed what he did. Although the preparation took longer than we anticipated, it was always worth it all once we sat down at the table to eat. Looking back on Daddy's preparation for this dish, I realize he took time to complete it with love, pride, and great detail. My brothers, our mother, and I benefitted greatly from my Dad's patience in cooking with love. (I would love to share that yummy recipe, but it will have to wait for another time!)

Everything in our society is rushed, from fast food to pre-packaged meals and text messages; we don't take time to give attention to our intentions. From people speeding in their cars to folks speeding through life, we see everyone rushing to get to the next place. It would be nice if we could go back to the "old days" and learn that anything worth receiving is worth waiting for because of the attention to detail within the preparation. This is all that God is asking us to do: wait upon Him and His timing.

I have a message for the single people reading this book: God has not forgotten about you. He knows how much you've desired someone to become part of your life. I'm sure this can be a very trying time in life for you; you're probably feeling like you will never find that special someone. But God is not a respecter of people; this means if He has blessed others in this way, He will do the same for you. Isaiah tells us, "Therefore the Lord waits to be gracious to you, and therefore He exalts himself to show mercy to you. For the Lord is God of justice; blessed are those who wait for Him" (Isaiah 30:18 NIV). In Lamentations 3:26, NIV we read, "It is good that one should wait quietly for the salvation of the Lord." Speak your heart's desire but do not give up on God's desire to bless you and give you His best. I believe within my heart that

God is preparing your significant other and you so you will be equally yoked. You must not settle on just anyone but let God provide the one He has been preparing for you. Trust God; He will never lead you the wrong way!

To the married folks reading this book: Sometimes you look at your spouse and you wonder where the romance went. It has been months since you have been intimate and you worry that he or she is cheating. You have stopped doing your best and being your best because you feel that he or she has given up on you. You pray every night for God to do something different, to change your spouse, or to let you free from the marriage. Don't do it. Do NOT get divorced. Unless you are in danger, you must finish the course set before you. Start looking your best and preparing meals like you did when first married. Find new ways to engage your spouse's mind and enter into conversation. Seek ways to do things together that allow you to be closer to one another and therefore closer to God. Do not give up until God Himself has said, "Enough." And remember when praying that God's love is enduring and He is a patient God.

Now that I have spoken those words over you, let's talk about your non-marriage-related dreams. What dream has God placed within your heart? What do you long to do? Earlier in the book, we talked about how sometimes your plans and God's plans do not align. When you listen to that still soft voice and truly think about your dreams, you will realize that God put them there. You will know because you can't go a day without thinking about this career or action. When folks engage you in conversation on this topic you sometimes feel as though you have spoken too long and too quickly. You would love to work full time doing this for a living, and even then would feel like you hardly worked after a 40-hour week. What is your true dream? The thing you wanted to be when you were a child preparing for the real world. What was it that completed this thought when you were younger: "One day, I will be a…"

Whatever your dream, whatever the passion that moves you to go higher and dig deeper, chances are God put it there if you are experiencing much opposition and discouragement. So far we have learned that you must be patient, persevere, and hang on to God because those are the foundational principles that will allow you to reach your dreams and see His plans in your life worked out. Your dreams are worth the wait and as you continue reading you will learn the tools you need to reach them. Take the night to reflect upon your dreams and ask God to reveal what is hindering you from being encouraged as you wait on God's best for your life. Ask Him to show you what is causing you to believe your dreams aren't worth pursuing.

Your Application is Approved

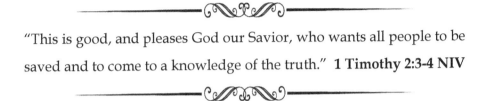

"This is good, and pleases God our Savior, who wants all people to be saved and to come to a knowledge of the truth." **1 Timothy 2:3-4 NIV**

How many times have you've applied for something and been denied? How many times have you thought you were going to land your dream job, have your offer accepted on the perfect house, finally get that credit card with all the great rewards, or earn that coveted spot on the Board of your local charity or league? How have you reacted when you were denied? Did you feel rejected, unworthy, as though someone else were controlling your life and affecting your future decisions? Be honest. Maybe you told yourself, "I'm tired of rejection. I'm not even going to try anymore." Or maybe you stopped pursuing your dream because you figured, "What's the use? They are just going to say 'No' anyway." However you reacted, I understand. I have been there too.

The application process itself causes you to feel vulnerable from the very beginning, whether you are applying for a credit card or new home, a job or a position on a local Board. You put your entire life on a sheet of paper and then turn it in to a complete stranger who will now critique it with a fine-tooth comb to determine if you are deemed worthy enough to pass his or her inspection. But that's not the end! Once he or she is finished and has determined that you are worthy, you have to pass through at least one or more other individuals depending upon the application's purpose and industry. It is daunting and can make anyone feel ready to quit before beginning.

What if I told you that unlike job applications, there is an application you can submit that only has one reviewer and for which you don't need any credentials beyond being you? Well, there is! There is a higher supervisor watching over us and He is waiting for you to submit your application today. The application that God gives us is the application for a fulfilled life. He wants us to benefit from all of His blessings. And what is most amazing about this application is that it is the master application – when you submit your application to God, you are asking that He have dominion over every future application you will submit. Bank officers, Human Resources professionals, home owners all come under His authority. When you are accepted by God, He will move mountains to ensure you have every door open to you that needs to open so you can complete His plan for your life. And everyone who applies is accepted!

Once we have been accepted by God, we will find that we still have to wait at times. His timing is best because He can see ahead of us and understands what is coming our way. Was your recent job interview met with rejection? There could be a better one coming in a few months that is not yet available. Someone has to quit so the position becomes open so you can apply for it. Or maybe He realizes that you and the boss will not get along and you will find yourself in a miserable position that causes you to neglect your other responsibilities, so He is saving you from that pain. He always knows what His plan is and when you submit to His leading, He will ensure you have His best in His time in His way.

It's an amazing feeling when we go to the Lord! He's already standing there with the love that only He can give to us. Keep a positive outlook on life and what comes with it, and although it may say one thing, God will allow only what's best for you. Your application to become part of God's family has been approved and you are ready for love, joy, peace, and fulfillment that are part of the benefits He offers!

Become Broken, Then Break Through

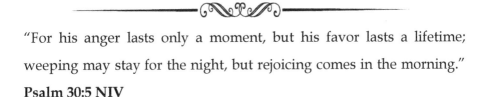

"For his anger lasts only a moment, but his favor lasts a lifetime; weeping may stay for the night, but rejoicing comes in the morning."
Psalm 30:5 NIV

Being broken is never a pleasant place to be. You begin to feel alone, like your spirit is down, or like no one can relate to or understands you! If you are in Christ, you can easily lose hope and your faith becomes consumed with doubt when the enemy attacks. You might turn to other things, such as negative energy (people). People will begin to tell you, "I told you serving God and going to church do not work. You might as well stop praying." It is important for you to understand that those around you can uplift you or tear you down with their words and the intent behind them. Both life and death are in the power of the tongue (Proverbs 18:21). Being broken is not a terrible thing; it is an opportunity for God to elevate you to your next level in Him. Some refer to this as the "midnight hour"; when it feels like all else is dark and there is no hope. But even at midnight, God is faithful!

Sometimes God has to take you through the broken stages so you can be stripped down before you fully understand that He is victorious and will save you from your situation in due time. When you are broken, God then has you in a place where He can reach you and begin to mend and correct all of the cracks, bruises, and tears in your life.

To experience breakthrough, you must first be willing to be vulnerable knowing that there are corrections that have to be made in your life. You must trust the process by allowing God to change your future, releasing the hurt and the blame, and discarding the baggage you have carried for so long. You must rebuke the lies, the put downs, disappointments, and guilt from the past that won't seem to let you go. God wants you to be complete and sometimes that means being broken to the point that you're completely open to Him. This is how He exposes and reveals what we are carrying on the inside.

In Matthew 9:20-21, we learn of a woman who has been bleeding for 12 years. She crawls through the crowd and reaches out to Jesus, touching the hem of His garment. As she does, He feels His power leave Him and turns toward the crowd to see who had committed this act. In verse 22, we read, "Jesus turned and saw her. 'Take heart, daughter,' he said, 'your faith has healed you.' And the woman was healed at that moment." When many read these verses they think of the woman's condition: her issue with bleeding for so long. But when I read this story, something else stands out to me. Give me a moment to share what I see.

This woman had been hurt. She had been rejected by people, cast aside, and looked down upon for so many years. She knew pain that you can only understand if you have experienced it. Sound familiar? Many of you can identify with this woman and her feelings of loneliness, rejection, abandonment. Imagine living year after year with that condition – one no amount of money could cure – then one day hearing that a man was walking through the city who possessed the power to heal you. That is what happened with this woman. She had no other hope; this was her only shot. That morning, she had to make up her mind to get to Jesus as any cost, including her life. And she did just that. Her willingness to reach out and get to Jesus regardless of how it affected her reputation, what boundaries she had to cross, or whether folks would stone her for going into the city with her illness. And because of her willingness, her faith healed her and Jesus pronounced her healed. (You can read her entire story in Matthew 9:18-26.)

One thing I have learned is no matter how fast the curve ball, how bad the situation hurts, or what people have done, God's perfect plan for our lives is worth it all! God determines what takes place and His directions are always precise. Don't seek man to speak a word over you, just to go forward; God's Word says, "I will never leave you nor forsake you" (Joshua 1:5) and "I can do all things through Jesus Christ that strengthens me" (Philippians 4:13). Because of this, you have the victory.

It is imperative to remember that Jesus himself had to endure the very things we are going through now. He knows all about the pain, being betrayed, and tears you've cried. Jesus will also heal your broken heart and give you the strength to forgive the ones who have broken it! When you go through a situation, you shall receive your reward if you faint not (Isaiah 40:31)! When Peter was on the boat and He saw Jesus walking on the water, he believed he saw a spirit. However, as Jesus got closer Peter knew it was his Master. Peter wanted to believe He could walk on the water like Jesus and he did until he took his eyes off Jesus. It was right as he took his eyes off the Lord that he began to sink and fear came upon him (Matthew 14:22-33). What does this teach us? As long as we keep our eyes on Jesus and be careful not to let the currents of life cause us to lose focus on Jesus, we can – and will – make it.

The woman with the issue of blood had been broken for 12 years and she suffered greatly, but her breakthrough came when she decided to no longer allow other people or her circumstances to stop her from getting to Jesus. Her healing came when she decided to go after her victory (Matthew 9:18-26). We have to go after our victory and let the enemy know that we are determined to come out triumphant. We can't let our circumstances or people stop us from attaining our breakthrough. Being broken before your breakthrough simply means that the pain is only temporary.

Are you currently thinking of giving up? Or do you feel like life will never turn out right? Do you feel like everyone else is succeeding while your life is mediocre at best? The enemy's job is to torment us and deal with the mind. He knows if he can destroy our spirits to the point of convincing us to give up or causing us to feel like no one cares, then He wins. The truth is the enemy does not come into your situation tiptoeing, he comes with force so he can hurt and confuse you. The Bile says, "He comes to kill, steal, and destroy" (John 10:10). We must not throw in the towel. God is our peace. We can take a stand and command the enemy to leave by speaking life into our dead situation and keeping our focus on Jesus Christ. The woman with the issue of blood focused on the garment. Peter focused on Jesus. This is the only way to pull out of that feeling of being weighed down. Remember this battle is not yours but the Lord's (1 Samuel 17:47). God is in not only in your corner cheering you on, but He is your number one fan. Romans 8:31 asks, "What shall we then say to these things? If God be for us, who can be against us?" It doesn't matter what the enemy says, does, or tries, he can't win. Begin to praise God in advance for the victory that is yours! Complete the battle; victory is yours and your breakthrough is near.

Just Wait

"But they that wait upon the Lord shall renew their strength; they shall mount up with wings as eagles; they shall run, and not be weary; and they shall walk, and not faint." **Isaiah 40:28-31 NIV**

You are at a corner, looking around it, waiting in anticipation on the change you've prayed for. It seems like it has taken forever and God has forgotten you. I want to encourage those who currently feel like there is no way out of their current situation. Just wait! Waiting on God can be sometimes difficult, especially when you are waiting for a mate or job. You begin to feel like you have been forgotten or aren't worthy to be blessed. But God is faithful and will give you the desires of your heart when you seek Him diligently (Psalm 37:4). He wants to make sure that when He blesses you, you are in the right position and can handle what He's blessing you with. 1 Corinthians 1:9 tells us that "God is faithful by whom ye were called unto the fellowship of his son Jesus Christ Our Lord." This means if you believe in his son Jesus Christ, and you are faithful to God, He will be faithful to you!

For example, if you're praying for a spouse and it seems like everyone around you has been blessed with a husband or wife except you, know that God hasn't forgotten you. I believe that we must be repositioned for purpose - God's purpose - which means we can't determine our plans. We have to be aligned up with His plan for our lives. There is a song entitled "Let Go and Let God" in which you learn that once we submit to His will and say to Him, "I surrender to it," God can then begin to open up the windows of heaven and provide you with an answer to the prayers you have been praying. Another thing that God wants us to do is just ask Him what it is we desire. Mathew 7:7 reads, "Ask and it shall be given you, seek and ye shall find, knock and it shall be opened unto you." The Bibles clearly says that all you have to do is ask. It didn't say how long it would take because God's timing is not our timing (Habakkuk 2:3).

We must ask God about our purpose and how can we be aligned with His will. I believe God has a mission for us all. We were not all called to preach but every job is equally as important. Being repositioned for His purpose should be our ultimate goal:

being a light in a dark world and making a difference in someone's life. This walk is not about us, it is about the Kingdom of God and His people! I have made up in my mind that if my call is to only be an encouragement to someone else's life then I shall give all glory to God for that purpose. I believe if we take the time to care for other's and be concerned for them, God will take care of our needs.

Remember to stay encouraged and not give up. It is almost always true that when one door closes, another one will open. Keep the faith and continue to wait on God. He's a God of love and compassion and He cares for you. He will come through for you. Just wait!

It's Time to Forgive

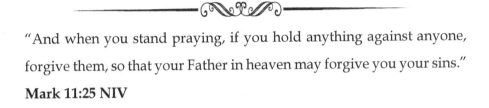

"And when you stand praying, if you hold anything against anyone, forgive them, so that your Father in heaven may forgive you your sins."
Mark 11:25 NIV

Let's take a journey more than 2,000 years back in time and think of when Jesus walked the Earth. Jesus, the Messiah, the King of Kings, was crucified on the cross and humiliated in a way none of us will likely know in this lifetime. He was belittled, spit upon, whipped, stabbed, and mocked. The Son of Man did all this for us so we could forgive others and have life to its fullest.

Can you imagine leaving your Father in Heaven and being asked to take on the sins of people who don't even believe you are telling the truth about who you are? Imagine what it must feel like to know you will be talked about, laughed at, and spit upon but you still have to stay focused on your mission. It happened to Jesus.

When faced with these realities, Jesus began healing them from their infirmities, casting out spirits, making the ultimate sacrifice for people who still didn't believe in Him. If you had a way to call Jesus and ask Him if He felt it was easy, I am sure He would say, "no but my love is greater than that alone so I paid it all just so you would have life and have it more abundantly." God sent Jesus so we would have someone to emulate our lives after. Jesus had to forgive them who were against Him then just like He forgives us now!

To move forward, you must forgive everything and everyone that may have caused you hurt, grief, or confusion. You must understand that forgiving and letting go is not done for others, it's for your benefit. If you don't forgive someone then that person still holds power over you! Luke 6:37 says, "Judge not, and ye shall not be judged: Condemn not, and ye shall not be condemned: forgive, and ye shall be forgiven." In other words: if we don't forgive, God won't forgive us!

Looking back over my life, I have learned that loving others regardless of whether they return it is rewarding. You don't have to worry. God promises that your enemy will be your foot stool (Luke 20:43). It is important to focus on the positive things that come out of the negative. There is always a lesson to be learned because God arranges your paths straight to your destiny! The only one you should be concerned about pleasing is God; and He will not only be there for you, but He will help you when you are in need!

Jesus showed how to let go and to forgive even after all of the hurt and betrayal He suffered. As Jesus was on the cross between the two thieves, He said to His heavenly Father, "Father forgive them for they know not what they do" (Luke 23:34). God uses negative situations to draw us closer to our purpose and destiny (Romans 8:28), so "count it all joy" (James 1:2-8) when you encounter struggle. He never allows anything if it isn't part of the plan. Jesus suffered greatly on His journey to the cross, but it was all part of the plan. You must be open to His plan and perfect will for your life. Tears will come, disappoints will occur, and struggle will be your reality at times, but know that there will come a time when, "Though you're tried in the fire you'll come out as pure gold" (1 Peter 1:7). Forgive!

Trust Again

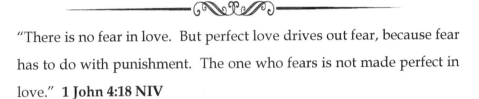

"There is no fear in love. But perfect love drives out fear, because fear has to do with punishment. The one who fears is not made perfect in love." **1 John 4:18 NIV**

So you have forgiven folks, now what? I understand you've been hurt and it's hard to trust again. Trusting someone is one of the main things you are finding it hard to do in your relationships because you question intentions and wonder what else is expected of you. Your past relationships have dictated how you go into new ones and you are feeling more alone than you ever have in your life, aren't you? If so, this chapter is for you.

Being hurt by people can cause you to feel as if you can never trust again. You may be in disbelief, feeling broken and hurt by others, and wondering how you will ever feel accepted when all you have experienced is rejection. This hurt can stunt your growth because you become stagnant and start to allow your mind to convince you that your moving forward is impossible!

"What have I done to deserve this?"

"I will never let my walls down again."

You become plagued by a fortress of darkness that you believe protects you when it is really harming you. These lies that you tell yourself only prevent you from becoming all you are purposed to be. They are lies from the pit of hell that the enemy uses to keep you from establishing the covenant relationships God has planned for you so you can reach higher and accomplish more than you ever have in your life. Remember the devil's only purpose for being is to destroy our ability to reach all that God has in store for us (John 10:10).

Please allow me to share an example of this principle walked out. In 7th grade, there was a girl who I believed hated me for no reason. She wasn't a bully; she just didn't like me. She would follow me and say things like, "You think you're better than everyone else, don't you?" She would tell me she hated my hair and say other things that were not polite or acceptable to others or me. One day, we were assigned to work in groups and act out our favorite TV commercial. Guess who was assigned to my group! Neither of us liked this fact. To compound the problem, several of my friends were also in my group and were not happy with how this girl had been treating me. Consequently, they decided to give her the silent treatment. Though I wasn't completely sure it was the right thing to do, I felt she deserved this because of the things she said and did not encourage my friends to stop.

One Saturday morning, my mother and I were running errands when we had to stop at a red light. I will never forget looking over and seeing the girl being slapped around by her foster mother. I never knew she was living that way and my heart instantly broke for her situation. She never saw me that day but I knew I could not let what I saw go unacknowledged. I knew I had to make a change that would help her not feel that way at school too. When we returned to school that Monday, I went out of my way to befriend her. I remember in her brokenness she asked me, "What is wrong with you? Why are you being so nice to me when I've been mean to you?" I told her I forgave her for how she was treating me and she shared that no one had ever done that before. She shared the details of her home situation and we became friends from that day forward. If I had gone back to school and shared with my friends what I'd witnessed, things could have gone differently and I could have caused damage to that young girl. Instead I helped her to see God's love walked out and help her trust again.

It's never a mistake when God sets us up for encounters in our lives. Similar to how my God had a different plan for my schoolmate and me. Although she seemed mean and demonstrated to me that she didn't care for me, we eventually became friends and she was able to experience God's love through me. God wants to use us as vessels to plant his seeds of love and bring change to those who have experienced hurt and have been mistreated!

We will encounter hurts. There will be reoccurring events that will tempt us not to trust the process of moving forward with others. However, just as Christ has demonstrated His love to us, we must show it to others. If you truly seek Him, God will grant you the courage to look fear in the eye and allow forgiveness to become a formula for your everyday life.

Leave the Past Behind

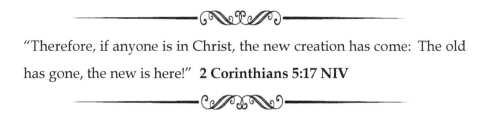

"Therefore, if anyone is in Christ, the new creation has come: The old has gone, the new is here!" **2 Corinthians 5:17 NIV**

According to Merriam-Webster (2015), the word past is defined as, "having existed in a time before the present: from, done, or used in an earlier time." Without saying many words, it basically means whatever was is now over; it's a new beginning. The word future is defined as "that is to be; of, relating to, or constituting a verb tense expressive of time yet to come; existing or occurring at a later time" (Merriam-Webster, 2015). Oftentimes, people hang on to the past without even knowing it. Are you one of them? I think we all can relate to this subject of realizing that the past is gone and we are living in the present. The repercussions of living in the past can be dangerous and can cause great pain. Allowing the past to control your future will make you feel like it's all over, and if you're not careful it will stunt the hopes, dreams, and the visions God has placed within you.

The good news is that Jesus will give you a new beginning. Whatever took place that was negative will be erased. God is saying it's time to move forward into your promise, just as the song says, "The wait is over, because it's your season" (Donald Lawrence, 2009, *Seasons*). You're still here and God's given you another chance. Philippians 3:13 says, "Brethren, I count not myself to have apprehended: but this one thing I do, forgetting those things which are behind, and reaching forth unto those things which are before, I press toward the mark for the prize of the high calling of God in Christ Jesus." I encourage you to not look back but to look forward. Be excited about your future and the great things the Father has in store for you.

Isn't it wonderful that we serve a God that doesn't judge us or hold against us what has taken place in our past? He loves us so much that He steps in and wipes all of the negative things we've endured away. God restores the joy that was once lost, and replaces the sorrow with His love (Isaiah 61:3)! God has no respecter of people; He cares for us all the same. He will help you transition from the past into your future. Will you let Him?

God wants to be your everything. He desires to transform the negative past into something beautiful! Don't worry about things, trust God to live out Romans 8:28, and know that "all things work together for good to them that love God, to them who are the called according to His purpose!" It is essential to leave room for joy, peace, and happiness in your life. Be careful not to dwell so much on the negative. Striving to walk out your purpose means letting go of your past. My mother used to always say, "God has a miracle in motion for you. You may not see it, but it's on the way."

Remember you are an important part of God's plan. God has placed many gifts within you, and He wants to see you be successful! Let the past go and live in the present. Go after what God has for you; and if you should fall, get up and keep going. Understand the fullness of what you possess and who you are, then act accordingly! Embrace your yesterday, for without the trials of your past you would not have the tools to conquer the trials of today. Without fail, you shall recover it all!

Thank Judas for the Kiss

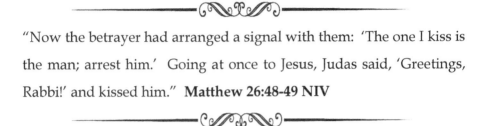

"Now the betrayer had arranged a signal with them: 'The one I kiss is the man; arrest him.' Going at once to Jesus, Judas said, 'Greetings, Rabbi!' and kissed him." **Matthew 26:48-49 NIV**

God's plan is never a mistake, although sometimes we don't understand it. We all have people placed in our lives, some for a lifetime and others for a season. Some folks bring you joy and support you to the fullest; others bring hurt, pain and betrayal. Although the pain they bring has hurt you, and the betrayal was real, it was all for a purpose. Look for ways to understand what His purpose is by reflecting upon the last time you were hurt.

You may remember that Jesus had a close friend betray Him. For Him it was someone He spent a lot of time with, poured life into, and kept within His close circle of confidents. Why did Judas betray Jesus? We know that Judas was chosen to be one of the 12 disciples, and although Judas wasn't as close to Jesus as the others, he still spent time with Jesus. He knew Him, he witnessed the miracles that Christ performed, he heard the Gospel being delivered from Jesus to others who believed. Did Judas even believe Jesus to be the true Messiah? Out of all of the disciples he was the one who called Jesus "Rabbi" or "Teacher" most often, basically only acknowledging Jesus as a teacher or leader but not the Messiah. We may never know these answers, but we know that Judas issued the ultimate betrayal: one that led to Christ's crucifixion.

When you read the Gospel according to John, it appears that Judas was a pretty selfish person who only cared what he could gain, and would do anything to ensure his own success. But what was the real reason Judas betrayed Jesus, and why with a kiss? I believed Judas was used as a vessel to get Jesus to the cross. Yes it was very deceiving on his behalf; it was the worst form of backstabbing and betrayal any man will experience.

Before Judas was born, God had a purpose for him and it was to get Jesus to the cross so He could die for our sins. God's will was for none of us to be lost, and because Christ died for us, we all can have a new beginning and eternal life. As harsh this all may have seemed Judas' purpose was great. Can you think back on an incident with a person who betrayed you? Think back to someone who hurt you so bad you were left picking up the damaged pieces. I want you to understand that the same reason Judas betrayed Jesus is the reason those who hurt you did so. You have your own destiny to reach, and without your Judas and their betrayal, you wouldn't (or won't) come out of the test as strong.

Sometimes people enter our lives in passing. They're not meant to stay but their purpose is beneficial to God's plan concerning us. The Bible says in Luke 22:47, "While he was still speaking a crowd came up, and the man called Judas kissed Jesus to identify Him to the soldiers, so they would know who to arrest."

So I say to you today, if you're a spouse and you've experienced betrayal, or even a co-worker did some under minded things to you just to benefit themselves on the job, or you have a bad experience with a friend who has lied, tell them thank you for the kiss of betrayal. That kiss is only getting you to your next level. It's God's strategic plan to use them for you!

Jesus knew that Judas would be used to serve the purpose, to get him to his destiny. We have to recognize people who play that role in our lives. Yes, betrayal can hurt you. Although Jesus already knew that Judas would be the one to betray Him, I'm sure it hurt Jesus to feel and witness this. He knew, however, that God's will needed to be accomplished and He accepted the pain and continued on His path. If you experience betrayal (and if you haven't I'm sure you will at some point in your future), remember to remind yourself to rejoice in the Lord for what He's doing on your behalf. Christ struggled, and the disappointments He experienced were just a demonstration to us that we can take it and we will make it. Your purpose will surpass your heartaches and the betrayals you've experienced; and one day you will experience joy unspeakable. As long as we live, we will suffer and experience hurt, confusion, and betrayal; but it is important to remember that none of it will be in vain. You will look back on each experience and see how you came through them. Yes, another trial will come; but you'll gain knowledge from each experience and will come out better than you were before. Remember that greater things are coming for you! Tell your Judas, "Thank you for the kiss!"

Hear the Call

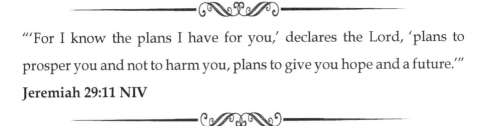

"'For I know the plans I have for you,' declares the Lord, 'plans to prosper you and not to harm you, plans to give you hope and a future.'"
Jeremiah 29:11 NIV

Have you heard the call? To me, the call represents being noticed or called for a task or purpose. Consider for a moment what it means to you – to be called to something? I wonder if most of us know or realize how valuable or important we are to God's Kingdom work, or how He desires to use us to complete His plan. The Bible consistently talks about someone going out on a journey for God or Him using them to deliver a message and so forth. This still applies today. God isn't looking for you, He has already found you. The gifts you have, He placed them there!

Do you remember when you were younger and your mother would stand at the door and call your name when it was time to come in from playing outside? You would answer when she called (or at least I hope you did). By answering your mother, you knew that you were obeying a voice that was of importance to you. You also realized that what happened when you answered the call wasn't always predictable – sometimes you had a phone call, other times dinner would be ready, and then there were the times when you didn't do something you were supposed to do and you had to go running to ensure she didn't become more upset! Whatever reason she called you each of those times, you can look back and see how each was beneficial to you! It is imperative that you don't get caught up in positions and titles or what people think. You should not be allowing them to take your focus away from what God Himself has called you to do. Just as you wouldn't expect other children to have run toward your mother when she called your name as a child, you should not expect that everyone will understand the call God has given you.

It is easy to get caught up in other people's opinions of what you are doing, but God spoke your name not theirs. I believe that we all are placed here on this earth for a reason but my reason may not be the same reason you're here; in other words, "We can't all wear the same shoes because we all wear different sizes." When we try to fit someone else's shoes it can become very uncomfortable.

At the beginning of a basketball quarter, the Center's job is to stand in the middle and jump the highest to try to swat the ball toward their teammates. Why would you try out for that position if you can't jump? Instead, you would try out for a position that best uses the skills you have. Whatever you try out for, every position on the team is vital and necessary to win a game! Play the position God has called you to and you will be successful and fulfilled. Play another one and you will always feel like you are coming up short.

God's call can come to you through a dream, a thought, a tug at the heart, or in a feeling of heaviness. For me, the call came by me not sleeping for many nights due to a feeling of heaviness on my heart. Once I answered the call, I felt like the weight had lifted. It can happen in many ways; but whatever way He calls you, be sure to answer. Don't worry if you're qualified or even if you can finish the task – just trust Him!

Moses is a great example of a person called by God who didn't think he was good enough to complete the task. He had a stuttering problem and was very embarrassed and shy. That didn't matter to God. He simply reassured Moses that He would be by His side. God knew Moses' future and knew that He had something special planned.

Have you felt like Moses before? Maybe you felt like you couldn't speak well or that you weren't right for the job? The whole beauty is that God knows all of your strengths and weaknesses – every one of them – yet has set you up to be victorious. He will either heal you, help you overcome the concerns, or will use them to your advantage and as part of your testimony. Don't you love God? You have to get into a place where you are focused on the call God has for you. Will this be easy? No, it won't! Will everyone support you? No, they will not! But knowing God's carrying you like we read about in the poem "Footprints in the Sand" (Stevenson, 1939), you can rest assured everything's going to be alright. Although you may be uncertain about the call, understanding that you're purposed to for the job will help you overcome all hurdles along the way.

Rise from Turmoil to Triumph

"For I am sure that neither death nor life, nor angels nor rulers, nor things present nor things to come, nor powers, nor height nor depth, nor anything else in all creation, will be able to separate us from the love of God in Christ Jesus our Lord." **Romans 8:38-39 NIV**

You are reading this book because something in your life isn't right. Something feels like it just can't go right, no matter how much you try. But you can rise from turmoil to triumph just like Joseph and so many of our forefathers did! Maybe you have been asking God, "What have I done?" Maybe your money seems to decrease each month and everyone is acting up in your life. Maybe your job is causing you more stress than you knew it would, or your home life is not going well. There are so many reasons to feel like you are in a pit that I could write an entire book on the subject, but let's keep moving forward. I have some truth for you that I want you to fully understand and let soak into the core of your being: **It does not have to be like this**!

You haven't done anything wrong. This is just how life works – you will have good days and bad days, joyous months followed by months when you feel like God has left you in the desert and forgotten about you; times of celebration as well as times of disappointment. I can relate to this feeling firsthand due to dealing with illness in my family. My Grandmother (Madia) passed away. I lost a sister-in-law who was like a sister to me. My father died a short time later. And now my mother is ill. As I write this book and share these tools with you, I am speaking to myself as well as to you. I am running this race with you.

One day when things felt like they were overwhelming me and pushing me past my limit, my eldest brother explained to me, "Kim, when you get to this part of life – dealing with your parents' aging and getting ill – it is a very hard place to be in. The family starts to feel very overwhelmed, they start to have disagreements. It is not because they don't love each other, but it's the stress of it all. Truth is... it down right hurts, experiencing this and watching the people you love dearly suffer; but it's just life!" It was then that I truly understood that I was not exempt from this experience and that I'm not the only one experiencing this. I certainly won't be the last. It is important to remind yourself that you are not in this alone. We all must walk a road that will be difficult to travel at times. You must go through something if you want to come out and share a testimony of victory!

Turmoil; what a word! Webster (2015) describes it as "a state of confusion or disorder." Turmoil can change your attitude; a typically positive person may find themselves being extremely negative. The very existence of who you are can change if you allow turmoil to have its way! This is the time you have to place things into perspective and ask yourself, "Am I willing to allow this thing take me over? Or am I going to take control over it?" There are four steps to take to get back on track:

➢ Breathe deeply.
➢ Pray fervently.
➢ Listen intently.
➢ Act accordingly.

God is your peace in the midst of the storm. You must regain control and realize that turmoil is just your current circumstance; it does not define who you are. Now it's time to pick up your pace and begin running victoriously toward the triumph you know deep down you were created to experience.

Triumph: the word itself sounds as if you're floating on air! It sounds empowering, "to conquer and be established" (Merriam-Webster, 2015). You must make up in your mind to change; once you do, you will gain the power to correct the negative things that await you.

It's critical to ensure you encircle yourself with positive people. If you have friends that bring negative energy, get rid of them immediately! You must understand that there are some people who will thrive in turmoil; in fact, they enjoy it! Pray and ask God for a positive support system in your life, and He will give you the people you need to be successful!

Your Purpose Awaits You

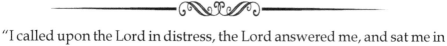

"I called upon the Lord in distress, the Lord answered me, and sat me in a large place, the Lord taketh my part with them that hate me."
Psalms 118:5 NIV

What are you waiting for? Are there goals and dreams you have, or a vision turning inside? Perhaps you want to return to school or change your career. Step out in faith; it's not too late. You can do it!

I have a mantra I call the three C's: Choice, Choose, and Change. You make the choice to enter into another chapter of your life with a positive attitude, then choose to have a positive attitude while you do it (even in the tough times), and allow God to change the atmosphere for you as you move forward. Place your hope in God, not man, and you will triumph over your enemies (Psalm 23). It is better to trust in the Lord than to put confidence in man (Psalm 118:8). Believing in yourself is half the battle. Allowing God to completely take over your circumstances will lead you to victory.

Reposition Yourself to Win

"But I have raised you up for this very purpose, that I might show you my power and that my name might be proclaimed in all the earth." **Exodus 9:16 NIV**

Wow! What a journey! Now that this book has reminded, demonstrated, and prayerfully encouraged you to walk into your destiny, you may be wondering, "What are the next steps?" We've talked about many things, from being patient to forgiving others, from letting go to walking triumphantly with God. Spiritually, you are almost to the finish line. How can you reposition yourself to win? Trust and depend upon God, change your thought process, and be open to His plans and will for your life.

I've said it before and will continue to remind you: You were born with purpose. Every tear you've cried, heartache you've felt, and disappointment you've experienced was not a mistake. You have not missed a beat; it all happened because God had a purposed plan with your name assigned to it. You have a great assignment ahead and only YOU can do it. Walk into your destiny and complete your task with confidence. The winds may blow and the branches on a tree might bend, but those branches don't always break. Don't let life's winds blow you down; instead allow them to help you grow and continue to learn. Stay focused on what's ahead of you and don't worry about how it will pan out. The way has already, been made.

Meet Me at the Finish Line

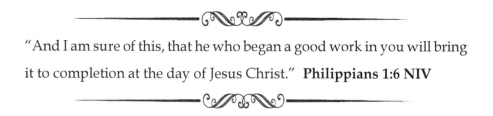

"And I am sure of this, that he who began a good work in you will bring it to completion at the day of Jesus Christ." **Philippians 1:6 NIV**

Now that you realize that God is in control, allow God to minister to you. Develop an even closer relationship with Him so He can align you with your purpose. Turn the negative into a positive and commit to loving yourself even more because of the value your life possesses. Take a deep breath and remember that a race is only won by those who are focused and determined.

As you move forward, know and believe that your better days are before you, and be encouraged to finish your race! It is time to step out on faith and do something that you've never done before. Don't worry about the outcome. Instead know that if it's meant to be, it will come to pass.

Do you remember the exchange between Pilot and Jesus in John 19:11? This is when Pilot said to Jesus, "Speakest thou not to me? Knowest thou not that I have power to crucify thee, and have power to release thee?" Jesus answered, "Thou couldest have no power at all against me. Except it were given thee from above." Jesus knew that His Father had placed Him there on a mission and because of who His father was Pilot's words carried no power.

We have to know who we are and whose we are; our Heavenly Father is in control of everything. Changing our thought process is vital to our success. If we believe that we'll never succeed, we never will. But if we speak life in everything we do, then good things will begin to happen because our mindset will always be positive. This does not mean we will never experience trials or that our race won't have hurdles, but it does mean that we will be able to triumph because we will always see the finish line in front of us.

As we leave one another, I challenge you to apply all you have learned in this book. Keep it somewhere that you can review it in the future when you need a pick me up. Study it with friends and commit to encouraging one another. Don't walk away unchanged. Rather, walk away knowing you have a purpose, a mighty purpose. Lace up those shoes, pick up where you were when you left the track, and finish your race! See you at the finish line!

About the Author

This is an exciting new journey for author Kimberly Robinson Green. With a background Early Childhood Educational, Director and Owner of the Christina's Preschool Academy, she has found her newest love: writing. She has produced two books: her debut novel entitled, "Her Cry~ Her Prayer~ Her Praise," which was released last year September 2014; and her newest book entitled, "Encouraged to Finish," an inspiring self-help book encouraging others to complete the race of life and be successful in what God has called them to do. Being a mother of three and a wife to her husband David Green of 20 plus years, she still finds the time to help and reach out to others. Kimberly often says, "We are not on this life's journey just for ourselves, but we were placed here to make a difference and help others along the way. I am a servant."

Under her organization, WWAV, she's in the process of starting a group called Open Heart Ministries. This group will bring awareness and outreach services for young teenage girls, mentoring them into the right direction.

She loves to spend time writing and being creative in various capacities, as well as spending quality time with her family and friends. Her mentor is her mother Christine Robinson. Kimberly is a mentor, writer, and motivator, but above all God's daughter. She is excited about her future in writing and looks forward with sharing her gifts with the world!

Connect with Kimberly:

KimberlyRobinsonGreen@gmail.com
www.about.me/kimberlyg333
facebook.com/KimberlyRobinsonGreen
twitter.com/kimberlyprtlnd

Thank you to my Amazing Team

My photographer Trenelle Doyle (Trenelle V. Photography), you started this journey with me, and have been such a blessing to me. Thank you sweetie.

My make-up artist, world-renowned Abibat Durosimi (Tabiba Styles). Thank you for your gift, it's an honor. You're amazing.

My hair stylist Cher'e Nickerson (Studio Six Nine Hair Design), you're awesome. Thank you for everything!

My assistant Ms. Shamika Bishop, thanks for your support and backup when it's needed. You're amazing!

Thank you to my Sponsors

Ms. Carry Green

Mrs. Christine Robinson

Mrs. Simone Carter

Mr. Jeffery Graves

Mrs. Corine Graves

Thank you to my Great supporter's

My Love Temple COGIC Family

Ms. Paula Brewer

Mrs. Anita Bailey Huff

Mrs. Sharetta Yates

Ms. Steffani Jackson

Mrs. Alethea Jennings

Author Tamyara Brown

Author Kimberly Lee

Author Alvin L. A. Horn

Author Selena Polk

PLANNING MY RACE

PLANNING MY RACE

PLANNING MY RACE

PLANNING MY RACE

_____
_____
_____
_____
_____
_____
_____
_____
_____
_____
_____
_____
_____
_____
_____
_____
_____
_____
_____
_____
_____
_____
_____
_____
_____
_____
_____
_____
_____

Planning My Race

_____
_____
_____
_____
_____
_____
_____
_____
_____
_____
_____
_____
_____
_____
_____
_____
_____
_____
_____
_____
_____
_____
_____
_____
_____
_____
_____
_____

Planning My Race

_____

_____

_____

_____

_____

_____

_____

_____

_____

_____

_____

_____

_____

_____

_____

_____

_____

_____

_____

_____

_____

_____

_____

_____

_____

_____

_____

_____

_____

_____

_____

_____

_____

PLANNING MY RACE

Planning My Race

_____
_____
_____
_____
_____
_____
_____
_____
_____
_____
_____
_____
_____
_____
_____
_____
_____
_____
_____
_____
_____
_____
_____
_____
_____
_____
_____
_____
_____
_____
_____
_____

Planning My Race

PLANNING MY RACE

PLANNING MY RACE

PLANNING MY RACE

PLANNING MY RACE

PLANNING MY RACE

_____

_____

_____

_____

_____

_____

_____

_____

_____

_____

_____

_____

_____

_____

_____

_____

_____

_____

_____

_____

_____

_____

_____

_____

_____

_____

_____

PLANNING MY RACE

_____
_____
_____
_____
_____
_____
_____
_____
_____
_____
_____
_____
_____
_____
_____
_____
_____
_____
_____
_____
_____
_____
_____
_____
_____
_____
_____
_____

PLANNING MY RACE

Planning My Race

_____

_____

_____

_____

_____

_____

_____

_____

_____

_____

_____

_____

_____

_____

_____

_____

_____

_____

_____

_____

_____

_____

_____

_____

_____

_____

_____

_____

_____

_____

PLANNING MY RACE

_____
_____
_____
_____
_____
_____
_____
_____
_____
_____
_____
_____
_____
_____
_____
_____
_____
_____
_____
_____
_____
_____
_____
_____
_____
_____
_____

PLANNING MY RACE

_____
_____
_____
_____
_____
_____
_____
_____
_____
_____
_____
_____
_____
_____
_____
_____
_____
_____
_____
_____
_____
_____
_____
_____
_____
_____
_____

PLANNING MY RACE

_____

_____

_____

_____

_____

_____

_____

_____

_____

_____

_____

_____

_____

_____

_____

_____

_____

_____

_____

_____

_____

_____

_____

_____

_____

_____

_____

_____

_____

PLANNING MY RACE

_____
_____
_____
_____
_____
_____
_____
_____
_____
_____
_____
_____
_____
_____
_____
_____
_____
_____
_____
_____
_____
_____
_____
_____
_____
_____

PLANNING MY RACE

_____
_____
_____
_____
_____
_____
_____
_____
_____
_____
_____
_____
_____
_____
_____
_____
_____
_____
_____
_____
_____
_____
_____
_____
_____
_____
_____

PLANNING MY RACE

_____
_____
_____
_____
_____
_____
_____
_____
_____
_____
_____
_____
_____
_____
_____
_____
_____
_____
_____
_____
_____
_____
_____
_____
_____
_____
_____

PLANNING MY RACE

_____

_____

_____

_____

_____

_____

_____

_____

_____

_____

_____

_____

_____

_____

_____

_____

_____

_____

_____

_____

_____

_____

_____

_____

_____

_____

_____

_____

_____

_____

Planning My Race

_____
_____
_____
_____
_____
_____
_____
_____
_____
_____
_____
_____
_____
_____
_____
_____
_____
_____
_____
_____
_____
_____
_____
_____
_____
_____
_____
_____

PLANNING MY RACE

_____
_____
_____
_____
_____
_____
_____
_____
_____
_____
_____
_____
_____
_____
_____
_____
_____
_____
_____
_____
_____
_____
_____
_____
_____
_____
_____
_____
_____

PLANNING MY RACE

_____
_____
_____
_____
_____
_____
_____
_____
_____
_____
_____
_____
_____
_____
_____
_____
_____
_____
_____
_____
_____
_____
_____
_____
_____
_____
_____
_____
_____
_____

Planning My Race

_____

_____

_____

_____

_____

_____

_____

_____

_____

_____

_____

_____

_____

_____

_____

_____

_____

_____

_____

_____

_____

_____

_____

_____

_____

_____

_____

_____

PLANNING MY RACE

_____

_____

_____

_____

_____

_____

_____

_____

_____

_____

_____

_____

_____

_____

_____

_____

_____

_____

_____

_____

_____

_____

_____

_____

_____

_____

_____

_____

_____

Planning My Race

_____

_____

_____

_____

_____

_____

_____

_____

_____

_____

_____

_____

_____

_____

_____

_____

_____

_____

_____

_____

_____

_____

_____

_____

_____

_____

_____

PLANNING MY RACE

PLANNING MY RACE

_____

_____

_____

_____

_____

_____

_____

_____

_____

_____

_____

_____

_____

_____

_____

_____

_____

_____

_____

_____

_____

_____

_____

_____

_____

_____

_____

PLANNING MY RACE

Planning My Race

_____

_____

_____

_____

_____

_____

_____

_____

_____

_____

_____

_____

_____

_____

_____

_____

_____

_____

_____

_____

_____

_____

_____

_____

_____

_____

_____

_____

_____

PLANNING MY RACE

_____
_____
_____
_____
_____
_____
_____
_____
_____
_____
_____
_____
_____
_____
_____
_____
_____
_____
_____
_____
_____
_____
_____
_____
_____
_____

PLANNING MY RACE

_____

_____

_____

_____

_____

_____

_____

_____

_____

_____

_____

_____

_____

_____

_____

_____

_____

_____

_____

_____

_____

_____

_____

_____

_____

_____

_____

_____

_____

_____

PLANNING MY RACE

_____
_____
_____
_____
_____
_____
_____
_____
_____
_____
_____
_____
_____
_____
_____
_____
_____
_____
_____
_____
_____
_____
_____
_____
_____
_____
_____
_____

PLANNING MY RACE

_____
_____
_____
_____
_____
_____
_____
_____
_____
_____
_____
_____
_____
_____
_____
_____
_____
_____
_____
_____
_____
_____
_____
_____
_____
_____
_____
_____
_____
_____

PLANNING MY RACE

_____

_____

_____

_____

_____

_____

_____

_____

_____

_____

_____

_____

_____

_____

_____

_____

_____

_____

_____

_____

_____

_____

_____

_____

_____

_____

_____

_____

Planning My Race

PLANNING MY RACE

PLANNING MY RACE

_____

_____

_____

_____

_____

_____

_____

_____

_____

_____

_____

_____

_____

_____

_____

_____

_____

_____

_____

_____

_____

_____

_____

_____

_____

_____

_____

PLANNING MY RACE

_____
_____
_____
_____
_____
_____
_____
_____
_____
_____
_____
_____
_____
_____
_____
_____
_____
_____
_____
_____
_____
_____
_____
_____
_____
_____
_____
_____

Planning My Race

PLANNING MY RACE

PLANNING MY RACE

_____

_____

_____

_____

_____

_____

_____

_____

_____

_____

_____

_____

_____

_____

_____

_____

_____

_____

_____

_____

_____

_____

_____

_____

_____

_____

_____

_____

Planning My Race

_____
_____
_____
_____
_____
_____
_____
_____
_____
_____
_____
_____
_____
_____
_____
_____
_____
_____
_____
_____
_____
_____
_____
_____
_____
_____
_____
_____
_____
_____
_____
_____

PLANNING MY RACE

_____

_____

_____

_____

_____

_____

_____

_____

_____

_____

_____

_____

_____

_____

_____

_____

_____

_____

_____

_____

_____

_____

_____

_____

_____

_____

_____

_____

_____

PLANNING MY RACE

PLANNING MY RACE

_____

_____

_____

_____

_____

_____

_____

_____

_____

_____

_____

_____

_____

_____

_____

_____

_____

_____

_____

_____

_____

_____

_____

_____

_____

_____

_____

_____

PLANNING MY RACE

_____
_____
_____
_____
_____
_____
_____
_____
_____
_____
_____
_____
_____
_____
_____
_____
_____
_____
_____
_____
_____
_____
_____
_____
_____
_____
_____
_____
_____
_____

PLANNING MY RACE

PLANNING MY RACE

_____

_____

_____

_____

_____

_____

_____

_____

_____

_____

_____

_____

_____

_____

_____

_____

_____

_____

_____

_____

_____

_____

_____

_____

_____

_____

_____

_____

_____

_____

_____

PLANNING MY RACE

PLANNING MY RACE

_____
_____
_____
_____
_____
_____
_____
_____
_____
_____
_____
_____
_____
_____
_____
_____
_____
_____
_____
_____
_____
_____
_____
_____
_____
_____
_____
_____
_____
_____
_____

Planning My Race

_____

_____

_____

_____

_____

_____

_____

_____

_____

_____

_____

_____

_____

_____

_____

_____

_____

_____

_____

_____

_____

_____

_____

_____

_____

_____

_____

_____

_____

PLANNING MY RACE

PLANNING MY RACE

Planning My Race

_____

_____

_____

_____

_____

_____

_____

_____

_____

_____

_____

_____

_____

_____

_____

_____

_____

_____

_____

_____

_____

_____

_____

_____

_____

_____

_____

_____

_____

_____

PLANNING MY RACE

_____

_____

_____

_____

_____

_____

_____

_____

_____

_____

_____

_____

_____

_____

_____

_____

_____

_____

_____

_____

_____

_____

_____

_____

_____

_____

_____

_____

.